The Greek Anthology

GREG DELANTY was born in Cork, Ireland, in 1958 and lived there until 1986. He became a citizen of the United States in 1992, and retains his Irish citizenship. He now lives most of the year in Vermont, where he teaches at Saint Michael's College, returning to his Irish home in Derrynane, County Kerry, each summer. Delanty has received numerous awards including the Patrick Kavanagh Award (1983), the Allan Dowling Poetry Fellowship (1986), the Austin Clarke Centenary Poetry Award (1997), and a Guggenheim Fellowship for poetry (2008). He has received an Irish Arts Council Bursary, and his poetry is widely anthologised. Delanty is a past president of the Association of Literary Scholars, Critics, and Writers (ALSCW).

D1637972

Also by Greg Delanty

Poetry Collections
Cast in the Fire
Southward
American Wake
The Hellbox
The Blind Stitch
The Ship of Birth
Collected Poems 1986-2006
The New Citizen Army
Loosestrife

Special Poetry Editions
The Fifth Province
Striped Ink

Translations
Aristophanes, *The Suits* (*The Knights*)
Euripides, *Orestes*
Selected Poems of Kyriakos Charalambides
Selected Poems of Seán Ó Ríordáin

Anthologies
Jumping Off Shadows: Selected Contemporary Irish Poets
(with Nuala Ní Dhomhnaill)
The Selected Poems of Patrick Galvin
(with Robert Welch)
The Word Exchange: Anglo-Saxon Poetry in Translation
(with Michael Matto)

GREG DELANTY

The Greek Anthology
Book XVII

Oxford*Poets*

CARCANET

First published in Great Britain in 2012 by

Carcanet Press Limited
Alliance House
Cross Street
Manchester M2 7AQ

www.carcanet.co.uk

A CIP catalogue record for this book is available from the British Library

ISBN 978 1 906188 05 4 paperback
978 1 906188 12 2 hardback

The publisher acknowledges financial assistance from Arts Council England

Typeset by XL Publishing Services, Tiverton
Printed and bound in England by SRP Ltd, Exeter

Contents

Acknowledgements

Many of these poems previously appeared in the Academy of American Poetry's 'Daily Poem' series, and in *Agenda*; *Alaska Quarterly Review*; *Alhambra Poetry Calendar 2009*; *Archipelago*; *The Atlantic*; *The Battersea Review*; *The Best Irish Poems of 2007*; *The Best Irish Poems of 2008*; *Daedalus*; *Dark Matter*; *Fulcrum*; *Green Mountains Review*; *The Irish Times*; *Literary Imagination*; *Love Poet, Carpenter: Michael Longley at Seventy*; *New Ohio Review*; *The Oxford Anthology*; *PN Review*; *Poesia* (with translation by Antonello Borra); *Poetry Ireland Review*; *Poetry London*; *Poetry Review*; *The Raintown Review*; *Riddle Fence*; *Southward*; *That Island Never Found: Essays and Poems for Terence Brown*; *The Times Literary Supplement*; and *Tuesday*.

A small number of the poems were included in two other books, *The New Citizen Army* (2010), published by the Combat Paper Project, and *Loosestrife* (2011), published by Fomite Press.

I would like to acknowledge the John Simon Guggenheim Memorial Foundation for a Guggenheim Poetry Fellowship, which allowed me the time to write a number of the poems, and Saint Michael's College.

I would also like to thank David Curzon, Gail Holst-Warhaft, Christopher Ricks, Nicholas Rynearson, Judith Willson and all those who helped me to finalize this book. I want to remember and acknowledge Katharine Washburn, who originally directed me to *The Greek Anthology* not long before she unexpectedly died.

Where now is the memory
of the days that were yours on earth, and wove
joy with sorrow, and made a universe that was your own?

"To a Minor Poet of the Greek Anthology",
Jorge Luis Borges, translated by W.S. Merwin

ἡ Ἀφοπλίζουσα

γυνή τις–λέγοις ἂν ἀτρύφερον—παραστείχει
   ἡμέτερον δόμον. ἄρτι ἐγερθεὶς ἀγανακτικῶς εἶχον·
ἡ δὲ γαληνῶς μειδήσασα σῖγα
   λέγει· "ἴδου τὴν αὔγην ἡλίου ἐν λίμνῃ·
ἴδου κλύμενον ζωπυρούμενον ῥοδοδάκτυλον
   ξανθῷ πυρὶ· ὁδοιπόρων ἐν Ὁδῷ Βορείῳ ἅπαξ ἡσυχάζων,
ἀκούειν ἔξεστι ξουθοπτέρου πτέρυγας
   στρεφόμενας μετεώρου." ὀρθρίᾳ ἄλλη γαλήνη τόση
μ' ἠνώχλησε ἄν·ἀλλὰ ὡς ἄπλαστος
   ὁ τρόπος. αὐτὴν λάνθανω.
ἀφωπλισμένος δὲ ἀφίημι ταῦτα οἷς ἀγανακτῶ
   καὶ ἐπεὶ οὐδεὶς θεὸς συμφέρεται
λογίζομαι—οἱ ἄλλοι θεοὶ ἅπαντες ὄξος—ὅτι
   δεῖ νέον κόσμον ποιεῖν καὶ αὐτὴν ὀνομάζειν
Ἡσυχίαν ἢ Ἀτρεμὴν καὶ ἀναβιβάζειν Ἀλκυόνα
   καὶ κελεύειν Ἀφροδίτην,
Ἄρην, Ἀρτέμιδα, καὶ Δία αὐτὸν, χώρειν μὲν γυναῖκι ταύτῃ,
   ἐν μέσῳ δὲ καταστῆναι, ἢ κούφως παρέρχεται
ἡμέτερον δόμον ὀρθρίᾳ ταύτῃ ἀμβροσίᾳ.

Nikos Metapheron

Preface

The Greek Anthology, which consists of sixteen books, is made up of short poems ranging over a thousand years, beginning from the seventh century BC. The poems include a wide range of epigrams—amatory, religious, dedicatory, sepulchral, hortatory, declamatory, and satirical. In the early tenth century, Constantine Cephalas arranged the poems by subject matter into fifteen books in a single manuscript now at the Palatine Library in Heidelberg. The monk Maximus Planudes rearranged the poems in the fourteenth century, and added the poems of *Book XVI*.

This *Book XVII* adds to the original *Greek Anthology*. The arrangement of the poems is by author and in the non-alphabetic order they came in. In certain cases the author's name was unclear. The proem in Greek by Nikos Metapheron appears as the poem "Disarming" later in the book. Because of space we could not include the Greek on facing pages, but felt we should include at least one poem in Ancient Greek.

That the rhythm and register of these translations are generally the same is in keeping with the tenor of the Loeb translations, to which I am greatly indebted. As is the case with many single translators of anthologies of different poets, my translations tend to make the different voices sound uniform. Indeed, this book, with so many different poets, may well be served better by having various poets translate rather than one poet (I hear that a group of Greek poets has already started translating *Book XVII* into modern Greek). Perhaps, if there ever is a *Book XVIII*, then various poets will work on that.

I have taken liberties with these versions and, of the three categories of translation that John Dryden distinguished, "metaphrase," "paraphrase," and "imitation," my translations should be set under the last. As the late Katharine Washburn explains in the introduction to her anthology *World Poetry*, "imitation" is "a translation in which the poet works from the original but departs from words and sense as he sees fit, sometimes writing as the author would have done if he had lived in the time and place of the reader." With this in mind, I have pushed certain poems beyond the epigrammatic state. Since a handful of the poems from this book are inferior to others, or incomplete, I would like to add a fourth category to Dryden's taxonomy, and that is "betterphrase," in which the translator improves on the original.

A frequent query about *The Greek Anthology* is why many poets have Latinate names. The Romans considered Greek to be superior to Latin, and the language of culture, and therefore they wrote in Greek, but kept their Latin names.

Many of these poems have been published over the past decade, going back to issue 157 of *PN Review* (2003), where twenty-two of them first appeared along with a version of this preface. I have not included the complete *Book XVII* as I felt that the excluded poems were either inferior or repetitive. A number of the poems included have also been published under my own name, outside of the context and authorship of *The Greek Anthology, Book XVII*.

Greg Delanty
Burlington, Vermont
June 11, 2012

THE GREEK ANTHOLOGY,
BOOK XVII

GRIGOROGRAPHOS

The First Story

The email, telling a friend *we're not too bad considering*
        the state of the world, crosses the Atlantic
with the touch of a key. The leaves of an evergreen blow
        like a shoal of emerald fish returning to the same place.
A cardinal in his scarlet robes pecks the feeder.
        The bells of the Angelus ring from St Joseph's.
The Angel of the Lord declares unto Mary, the infant god
        of my childhood is back on earth again, the one
I've ceased to believe in, the lifebelt that keeps believers afloat
        in the storm of being here, issuing tickets to
the hereafter ever since that garden episode, the tall tale
        of our banishment concocted by some storyteller
who'd be so flummoxed we've taken it for gospel
        he'd say: "Look around you now. Behold, the garden."

Free Flow

The waterfall bathes "the feet of Mount Parnassus,"
which is how a local described these lower slopes
in the town of Delphi, calling to mind Jesus
washing the feet of his disciples before he
turned bread and wine into the body
and blood of God. This is no blasphemy.
The gods flow freely in and out of each other.

Recycling

If myths are frameworks, then any one person's story
    is made from a scrap heap: a Cyclops here,
Chimaera there, Asklepios one minute, Persephone the next.
    Each is like a bicycle put together from old parts:
a rusty chain, racer handlebars, mudguards, an odd tyre.
    When people see you their eyes say *what a hybrid,*
how weird, how cool, how funny, awesome.
    They laugh. It may even have a rusty bell or horn
to warn everyone "Get out of the way, pronto."
    Still it gets you where you're going. The wheels turn.

GREGORY OF CORKUS

From Acropolis View Hotel

I work on a rooftop beneath one of the wonders
      of the world. From where I sit you can see droves
enter the Propylaea; peer over the Odeion of Herod Atticus;
      mill like ants to the olive tree, the trophy of Athena,
up to the temple of the war goddess. The Parthenon
      overshadows the Shrine of Gaia. All in ruin.
I hold back, enjoy the sight from a comfortable distance.
      An ant scribe keeping track of the ants.

Below the Monument of Lysikrates

My son shouts up to our balcony from the Road of the Tripods
      that he's got a new flute, fingers a tune.
Gods and godlings perk up their ears: the terracotta statuettes
      lining the tourist shop fronts, the broken busts
about the Acropolis. Silenus shoulders the stage of Dionysus
      within sight of our window, Mopsus, Apollo, Athena
on high. Once again the victory of the choral festival
      is lifted on this ancient road.

Fall Out

Today I read a poet's elegy for his friend
    written forty years after he passed away.
It hurt me to read, how friendship still shone,
    a paradigm of friendlove, the jewel
in the crown of life. And I thought of you,
    and wished I was that poet, and you had died
in the good old days, and it was I wrote that poem
    to you, my friend, my sometime friend.

Party Piece

Often the get-together is unavoidable:
    a marriage, funeral, function.
You brace yourself, most people being more
    friendly acquaintances than acquainted friends
—even with the latter you feel more at ease meeting one
    at a time, tuning into each other's frequency.
You tire of shop talk, gossip, sport-babble,
    politics, nervy jokes you laugh at too soon.
Tell yourself not to drink too much or your party mask
    will slip as you balance on the social pergola,
or rather the unsteady plinth of society, the necessary base.

A Special Bond

Funny, heartening, to live for years in a town
      and know simply by sight this face or that,
to maybe nod the vaguest of hellos on a crowded street.
      Neither ever crosses the line,
the border into intimacy, freed
      from claustrophobic ties
fraught with squabbles, slights, rivalry,
      the regular pressure of close relations.
One feels a peculiar fondness for them. Whatever
      you do, don't attempt to chat, become friendly.
Stifle any such urge at bus queue or shop counter.
      Perilous it would be to shatter
such a special bond, this remote intimacy.

Company

A secluded table in a café affords me a modicum
        of privacy. I settle down to read, work
among clusters talking sport, politics, shop,
        whiling away time. It's easy to feel warmth,
love even, towards others from this vantage.
        My jacket reserves the nearest chair
for my imminent friend, putting anybody off
        sitting too close, starting up conversation.
My company has arrived, Solitude herself.

At a Table in New Moon Café

Three women talk about their men, boyfriends,
        crushes. Each looks beautiful.
One wears ponytails and, on her wrist,
        the tattoo of a star; another has shower-wet hair
scented with hyacinth; the third one sews
        (surely Clotho) without a glance at her handiwork.
They take no notice of me at a nearby table,
        invisible as a cab driver—my hair thinning.
Clotho says of one beau: "I'm really not gone
        on him. He's too nice." Said in earnest,
no irony intended. The others nod, don't laugh.
        I wish I had been privy to this conversation
thirty years ago. I, who always fell over myself
        being nice to women I longed for,
hardly ever ended up with. If only I'd known.

Old Flame

From Riverside Drive a cloud wraps the distant mountain in
    a mohair scarf, the type a woman drapes about her neck,
a female who jams words in my Adam's apple.
    The traffic is bottlenecked. The lights turn
from red to green and back to red. Too late.
    I notice my gray hair in the rearview mirror.
A woman strolls through my reflection. She is the image of one
    I vowed to spend my life with once. The traffic flows.
No going back now. Gone forever, sipping her takeaway coffee,
    her ambrosia this bitter morning. Oh, my cold
old flame, old muse. Daughter of Mnemosyne, cruel you
                                        are today.

The Wall

A playful dog races his image
        on the tide-laminated sand.
The ocean itself is too turbulent
        to be a mirror. I'm more like the sea,
at least today, more a turbid empty storm
        repeatedly battering on
the eroded Rocks of Whyness.

The teacher testing catechism—the one that opened
        with *Who made the World?*—was probably right
my first year in school. I irked him, raising my hand
        continually, attempting answers. I was always
a little too earnest. He pointed to
        the dunce's corner with "Face the wall, fool."

DEANOS THE BEARDED

Hey You

How do expressions appear when you're alone?
    If you could scrutinize a cheerful friend, loving father,
serene sister, it would be like observing a face
    as the person descends from Holy Communion,
or stands alone over a family grave; all the stranger
    for being familiar. Each countenance as disconcerting
as when you catch yourself in a mirror,
    though by then you're aware—
if you could look without forethought
    you'd wonder who that person is,
how sad, glum, odd that face. Turn away.

FRANKOS KAVALARIS

Reflection

We think too much of what people think, the shadows
     they cast that we see as our own,
imagined or true. Horses galloping the beach
     aren't bothered by their dark reflections on wet sand.
They don't need shadow-blinds like high-strung thoroughbreds
     for fear their adumbrations will scare them.
Let's forget the umbras cast by ourselves and others.
     Let's drop the shadow-blinds.

Rock Bottom

The god of life brings us down with a look,
      a comment, and we hit rock bottom. It could be worse.
From below you can make out skate hovering like hawks
      in the heavens, the anemone swaying
in zephyr currents, the angler fish casting his ignis fatuus bait
      from his forehead to trick innocents
into his diabolic mouth, the great silhouetted shoals
      flying like arrows shot from the bow of Poseidon
—the gods still fighting ancient battles beneath the surface.
      I am a crusty old lobster safe in my crevice,
brandishing a boxing glove claw, jabbing at all
      who venture near. God of life leave me here.

The God of Small Slights

The list of cuts that the sly god of small slights
      prompts people to inflict is endless: "You're always late;"
"You live in the lah-di-dah section of town rather
      than the hoi polloi side;" "You tip parsimoniously."
Slight slights often shot behind the shield
      of a joke. Each like a splinter in the foot
that you ignore, thinking nothing of the prick
      at first. As the day wears on
you curse, hobble about looking for a needle to pry it
      from the inflamed skin, the seed watered
by the niggling vexation that it's got so embedded.
      You swear next time you'll not
forget to tread softly, not forget to wear slippers.

PLUVIUS

Appreciation

We treat the god of rain poorly, curse
    the drizzle, shower, downpour, hailstorm, torrent,
the cats and dogs, the deluge that cleared the air
    accompanied by Lightning and laggardly Thunder.
You'd think such insults would be too much for the god.
    Maybe at times they are and he throws a tantrum
and catches us without an umbrella at a football match
    or picnic, no shelter in sight. But this god is soft
by nature. Long may he reign. We forget that without him
    we'd be minus the multitudinous shades of green,
the harvests of Demeter, the gifts, bounty he showers
    upon us. Bow down now before the god of precipitation,
this brooding cumulous god, the weeping god of the sky.

White Out

The day gets away from me. Nothing done
    and it's lunchtime, rushing to a meeting,
held up by white-out traffic, the snow
    calling a halt to the daily life-and-death tedium:
committees, bills, email, post. If we croaked today
    what difference would it make? I give up,
tell myself to wait till the traffic eases off.
    Park. Drop into a shop. Watch the snow
erase the world. It is good to throw
    your hat at it all, not turn up, be nothing, no one,
watch the snow fall, turn to a blank page.

IANIA THE SEER

Ye of Little Faith

People walk, slide, glide, hula-hoop,
        somersault and land,
making their mark, signatures, circles
        within circles, brief squiggles, doodles on the surface.
Some laugh, some are deadly serious: children, mothers,
        fathers, lovers, friends, loners. People fall,
get up again, and not just on the frozen lake
        beyond our window. Daily you walk
on water yourself. Have faith.

Body Surfers

Nothing like it, to catch a ride on the comber,
      the muscle of the breaker curls into a wing,
Hermes' flexed scapula. We bodysurf the ruffled feathering
      of the water's wonder,
both messenger and message in the pinioned thunder.

FERRIUS

The Immortalists

Youngsters climb the gorge, limber as goats, leap thirty feet
        into a pool no more than two yards wide
surrounded by sharp limestone outcrops.
        There's no room for error. I watch these high flyers
from the precipice opposite. I can hardly bear to look down,
        want to holler *Stop*, but know that kids don't listen.
Besides, should one diver take notice he might hesitate,
        a glimmer of fear his downfall.
For now they're immortal, the temporary immortalists.

Race

We lounge under the shade of an ash
    in a hotel compound on Lake Morey.
The indolent water laps the shore like an obedient dog
    licks its master, spittle-scum on the side of its mouth.
The lake floor is mushy, a slime of sand
    with strands of green weed.
The wetsuit children play games, frolic,
    screech from boats or diving boards.
Their lives are concerned with nothing now
    but sport. They run the three-legged race,
strapped at the ankle to their privileged lives.

MAKANNUS

The Fallacy Pathetic

There's something confused about the wind today,
    demented, unruly,
the bushes and trees not knowing which way
    to turn—a bit like yours truly.
That's such an easy schoolbook analogy;
    pathetic fallacy, projection, codology.
The wind is nothing but its own alien element,
    and besides, to someone else it might be clement.

DOGUS

Pearls

The first grit entered the mantles of our selves,
irritants telling us we're alone, we're afraid, we're alive
yet shan't be here forever; inducing us
into creating nacreous deities who promise safety,
pearly-gated Hereafters, realms
a mother might describe when her child asks:
"Where's grandma gone?" "To a happy mansion
beyond the cotton-candy sky." Or, these dark pearls
set us above all else, fooling us into the slaughter
and slavery of the blood and chlorophyll races
and not simply to eat of their flesh or make clothes
out of their pelts. We are ingenious in our ways.
Pearls with brighter, mother-of-pearl hues exist
as well within our hard shells: Listen, even here
in the kitchen, music lilts from a silver box,
notes from everywhere, played and sung
by souls long gone. Gone where? That we know not
seeds many a pearl. We lie, countless mollusks,
buried in sand or huddled together on rocky beds,
valves opening and closing, unable to fathom
what's above the surface of our murky firmaments.

Deities

Like light from a star back of the universe
our multiverse voice reaches you as you kneel
in the mosque, church, synagogue, temple of your selves.
DanaUranusYahwehJesuVoidus—you name us.
We are legion, as many as there are stars
in the firmament, many extinct, many still to emerge.
Our voice is a heliograph saying we want to stay,
do not destroy us, we are the light
shining from the deep space within your atoms,
having traveled so far to reach you, shape and shade changing
according to your terrain and lives. You've seen no less
in creatures: the leaf insect, the gecko,
the cocooning butterfly. We survive
as best we can in your diverse habitats.

Gaia's Inn

The owner informs us the inn's closed, summer's over,
    but we're welcome to a few beers, to sit on the deck.
We're sensible enough not to take any notice
    of the begging dog with a stick in his mouth.
Ignore him long enough and he'll give up
    just as the nagging mutt of weekday routine,
nitty-gritty responsibility, has left us be.
    Buoys tilt like planets, each with its own biosphere
of creatures and plants. Suds at the water's edge.
    It seems Gaia has washed her hands
of the motor boat, the jet stream harming her, the radio
    reporting the all-too-human news of the planet
heating up, that we, the only species which destroys
    its own habitat, is also the only one which creates gods.
The goddess reflects, "Ah, they've been deity-making forever,
    making something of themselves, *Homo importanticus.*
Let's cut them slack. Where would we be without them?
    Soon there'll be no one here. Let them alone for now."

Driving in Vermont

The trees descend from the mountains in plumes of leaf-fire
    that people travel thousands of miles
to admire, but few spot the god taking a break
    from Delphi. Nobody asks him to dish out prophesy.
Perhaps they're too afraid to find out what lies ahead.
    I bet he came on the urging of an Abenaki deity
in the egalitarian realm of the gods.
    Folk drive by, their radios reporting the weather,
last night's frost, baseball, the demise of the world
    in the umpteen ways we've devised. A few may comment
on the glorious light, everyone hightailing it to work. But now
    my job is to pull off Rt. 15 at Hyde Park and Centerville
and report this sighting. Who'd have thought the god
    of light would be seen in the Northeast Kingdom,
Apollo himself, on the lam from his Attic stomping ground.

Lapse
after Geryon Murfi

We say our fate is in the lap of the gods, pray
      to our deity, but the pantheon today stood up in dismay
          seeing us run out of control across the map.
The majority of them take flight
      to planets
of distant galaxies whose denizens allow them to sit about.
The bushed gods who stay stretch themselves out,
      take a millennial nap,
but not before they cast bets
      on whether Gaia, who is so sickly that she is laid out,
          will make it through or not.
          Not a godly lap in sight.

IONO THE DRAMATIST

Visiting the Delphic Oracle

We climb to the oracle that people
    visit from distant islands with their supplications.
Temple Hocus-Pocus makes us feel better,
    conjures answers, gives us hope. Hope may be
the god who, down the ages, has been most
    necessary. Where would we be without hope?
We're so inventive, so hopelessly clever.

In This Life

All certainty of eternity is out
    the door: Purgatory, Hell, Tartarus,
Heaven, Elysium, but now we doubt
    the certainty of such certainty also,
reaffirming the zonulet at the edge of Oceanus,
    the fog-shrouded Cimmerian land, or of Limbo,
the only uncertain states we shall certainly ever know.

DAN THE YOUNGER

Paradise

To be inside on a wet day, rain on the roof,
    the heavens opening, the diamond drops draping
the window. Nothing to do but hunker in, snug
    under the quilt, in the armchair
by the fire with a book, or watch a game,
    no pressure to cut the grass, oil the bike,
clean the car, run to the bank, jog, swim—
    freed from the taskmaster of good weather.

PATTIA

Inklings

Our 'un can't grasp the notion of size, convinced he can
     climb inside a toy bus, fit a football through a keyhole
—a regular phenomenon among toddlers. I've a hunch
     the child unconsciously recalls that first place
we're rumored to hail from, an Unplace
     where size means no thing, where we are
like squid, size and shape changing, before our souls enter,
     settle in corporeal cells. And in this sentence
of flesh, inklings of our squidsouls leave us for dead
     in the ink cloud, having vamoosed back,
off, away, beyond into the lost Universe of Unsize.

MOSIUS THE ASTRONOMER

The Event Horizon

Perhaps those zones where our souls are said to end up
    are possible: that region the good inhabit, the one
where the imperfect are burnished perfect, the infernal place
    of no-hopers. The afterlife is no more unbelievable
than us landed here on this giant spinning-top
    whirling crookedly through space,

especially now the brains proclaim zones
    where time's altered, kaput; dimensions where stars slip
through self-generated cracks in space and so much more
    not dreamed of in our reality. Truly, after all, the soul
may have somewhere to go beyond the only event horizon
    we know of, our point of no return. Unbelievable.

Above the East River

The suspension bridge is a great hammock.
    If we could see other dimensions
we'd behold the god of ingenuity, Hephaestus,
        swinging ever so gently, slumbering above the traffic.

Imagine

We raise three inches of cordless chromium
     and natter with someone across the world
in another time zone. We've long outdone
     the gods, even Hephaestus and his inventions.
Picture someone long dead,
     brought back from the underworld,
taking in the whole show, scratching his head.

Market Morning

Mouffetard, surely a street straight out of paradise,
     Heaven, Elysium, those myth spheres
I don't believe exist except upon earth. So, this
     is it, the ancient thoroughfare
between Lutetia and Rome, on a Saturday morning.
     Especially now Helios is out shopping
along with everyone else. Fingers check the pears,
     pick up ruby-red wine, gold bars of bread, bronze pies,
jade olives, amethyst grapes. Such a bonanza. Us lounging,
     blowing on frothy bowls of piping café au lait.

Say I'm Wrong

Forget happiness. Accept your lot
        of mundane discontent,
family foibles and furies, the doldrums of friendship,
        the megrims of the body, not having an iota
regarding the whole show: the general epicedium
        since the human episode began.
Unhappiness is our plasma. Consider
        for instance the way you're more at ease, wallow
in Melpomene's sad songs. Consider the dearth
        of joyful emanation and say I'm wrong.
Maybe only then will Happy grace us.
        When we let go of his shirttail
this deity will begin to feel ignored, left out,
        tap us on the shoulder, say, "Remember me, pal?"

The Lesson

It's as though the god of unhappiness, of discontent at least,
        injected his serum in our veins when born, inoculating us
from feeling good for long. He's like a grim schoolmaster
        patrolling the playground, reminding children
they have only a minute or two before the line-up bell,
        darkening unconscious happiness, marring natural mirth
with back-burner anxiety, fretful they'll have to line up soon
        and march back into interminable lessons, tests,
right and wrong answers, punishment, the classroom's gloom,
        learning by rote, the slow tick of the metronome,
the dolor of the adult world, that life isn't *all* play.

LONGLIUS

Wish You Were Here

As we drove through the countryside, dry
       as the donkey's back that a grizzled man rode
into the infinity of the mountains, nothing was
       so spectacular as the purple and white oleander
a local called *pikrodaphne*, nonchalant
       about that picture-postcard flower lining the roadway.
His eyes are dulled by what is
       under the purview of the god Familiarity. If only
we thought of ourselves as tourists riding our planet,
       circling our heavenly star, writing postcards to ourselves,
beginning with: *Having a wonderful time. This place*
       is paradise, truly out of this world.

Road Workers

I only noticed them and then almost too late
    —as we drove on, cursing the minor holdup—
the laborers as they perspired in orange jackets,
    pouring tar, working dinosaur diggers,
one with an insect-eater snout. Maybe it was Maria Callas
    on the radio that opened up the sacred,
brought me to my senses, the high way of art.
    There they were, the Lares of motorways,
laboring away, laying out ink-black tarmac
    in boiling sun. Sweating for us beneath hard hats.

MONTAGUS

Prelapsarian

The satyrs of the cottonwood trees spurt,
    shoot seed into the air all over the city
without embarrassment, being branded indecent.
    How lucky they are, how unselfconscious
these swingers of plants, these exhibitionists.
    Another tree before the Fall.

BILLIUS THE LAUREATE

Silence

The workers renovating our neighbor's house
     blare heavy metal, even after I ask them to turn
it down. The electric strings screech, howl,
     the Furies themselves. Should Silence grace us
I think we would be unprepared, undone
     in her company. She would have us face ourselves,
the selves we divert and shroud out with noise:
     music, talk, laughter, whistling. Silence waits
to surprise us, expose each keen aloneness.

IOANNIS PICTORIS

Chronicle

for Jimnasium

Bells ring all across Sunday morning.
    People are summoned to their gods.
Even to a nonbeliever the bells
    are sacred: the peal, the carillon,
the pistillate chimes of swaying metal flowers.
    The bells toll, loll soothing
as a foghorn, train whistle in the distance,
    hoot of a ship sailing into harbor.
Such sounds chime our sole divinity,
    intimations of humanity.

NIALLOS THE TEACHER

Music of the Spheres

Eris visits us in different guises every day.
She comes now via the tyranny of Muzak
everywhere we go: the mall, bus, street, café;
rock, reggae, rap, jazz. For earth's sake,
drowning out the nothing sound. Almost everyone fears
the sirens singing this silent music of the spheres.

To a Teacher

especially for Iono the Dramatist

Once more you stand before a cabal of epheboi,
instructing them how to look at the sun.
You pin-hole a sheet of paper.
The light is blacked out, then emerges
out of the night of the moon.
                        Some pupils observe,
lit by learning, others show
not a glimmer of interest. How
can you guide them away
from eclipsing Acedia, Confusion,
Mammon: the dark gods of our day?
You bow your head as if before a shrine
reaching to set a candle alight.

Teenagers

They loiter, smoke, giggle, strut, cat whistle,
		shout obscenities, text, ogle
each other's crushes, torpedo into the Aegean.
		We hadn't heard school was out today,
curse these adultlets bursting with hormones,
		embarrassing to see as their acned faces,
their bodies sprouting hair. Don't be too
		hard on them. They're in
the cocoon agony, miserable, mortifying,
		alone. Ignoble to recall
even in old age. We should be kind,
		kindest of all to these. Spare them.

Terminal

And so, Tithonus, you're hooked
  to ventilator, catheter or cannula,
gagging down another pill, unable to fend for yourself.
  You pray to be released from the drip
as malignant cells metastasize,
  make nothing of you. Dawn even
abandons you in the snug-as-a-coffin terminal room.
  Nurses turn you, change your diaper.
You're unable to recall your own name,
  remember you can't remember,
eternally aware dementia erases the spool.
  The gods, as usual, show no mercy.

ROSANNA DAEDALUS

In a Diner Above the Lamoille River

The rocks below on the river trail foam fins
    as if they swim upstream along with the salmon
returning to their spawning grounds, leaping falls, freshets,
    whirlpools, the ancient anonymous struggle.
The fish age instantly to mottled old-timers,
    dying in the nursing pools of their birth waters.
A tour group of elderly are the only other diners,
    their skin mottled not unlike the salmon.
They seem to get along. They jaw about the weather,
    the water height, the amount to tip.
One woman's trembling hand fills the patron questionnaire
    with praise. I scribble this on the back of mine,
and tip the kind waitress a little more than usual.
    She laid their steaming bowls like a priestess setting
her libation on the altar of trembling elder gods.

Childhood

You wax lyrical about childhood being idyllic,
      a country under a spell:
a beach ball in the air, an uncle with the trick
      of a penny up his sleeve, a lick
of ice cream, blithe waving from the horses of a carousel
      galloping the hills of childhood. Well,
okay, but look again while the impaled horses circle.
Their faces suggest they're being whipped through Hell.

No Man's Land

Each dawn we struggle over the top
    of a regular day,
stumble on the barbed wire,
    the strewn bodies. Who'll cop
it this time? A brother? Friend?
    The bodies drop on all sides,
battling to the bunker of tomorrow.
    Our nerves so frayed
we begin to wish for our own end.

Eventually

ton koimismenon

The pot of grief,
all that is left of you,
bubbling on the blue flower
of a slow flame,

left there evaporating,
slipping the mind,
the water
all
but boiled off.

A New Law

Let there be a ban on every holiday.
       No ringing in the new year.
No fireworks doodling the warm night air.
       No holly on the door. I say
let there be no more.
       For many are not here who were here before.

IOUDITH EIKONOPLASTIS

Special Days

Give us the regular day any day,
not one hyped up, brimming with expectation:
a wedding, bank holiday, birthday, Christmas.
We *must* enjoy the gifts, new clothes, family.
The tyranny that we're supposed to be grateful
for the bounty of victuals, flavored
by the sauce-thought of those starving elsewhere.
Spare us such a day leavened with despair.

News in Flight

We fly over the city. The screen flashes current news.
        Nothing, it seems, but killing and mayhem.
Daily we're brought low, how far we've fallen.
        Hardly anyone says a word. Urban lights stretch into
the rural night below. Even fewer mention such wonders.
        The lights are like those of fans at a concert
holding up candles to their god, *Homo sapiens*,
        fleeting as any. Yet gods nonetheless,
bearing mayhem on the one hand and marvels
        on the other, as is the way of any band of gods.

At the Bar in The Daily Planet

The gods are always at it, picking on each other,
Hera and Poseidon, Hades and Demeter; more human
than the humans themselves, or at least
that's the way it seemed, till today it struck me
as the barman jabbed at a regular with a barbed remark
and turned up the news, everyone glued to the latest Iliad.
It is humans who put the gods in the shade,
being such expert backstabbers, naysayers, killers.
Too late even for a *populus ex machina* to save the day.

The New Opiate

Such skill with a ball, club, missile in the air.
Each side prays to their god to annihilate
the opposition; to slaughter them, fair
or unfair, with something close to hate.
The players substitute the deities who are dead.
The crowd's roar deafens. The gods go head to head.

BARRAS

After Listening to the World News Again

So, these days one is dimly consoled with the thought
Hell, even the sun will eventually come to naught.

Entering the Acropolis

In the temple of Athena Nike, the goddess smiles smugly
    down on the daily tourists in their comfortable Nikes.
She has won again. Not all victory is a matter of war. Complicity
    is the deity hardly anyone sees.

Names

Soldiers carved their names
    on slingstones: Gregory, Hipponik, Dan;
or words like *Ouch*, *You're Dead*, or *This Maims*:
    precursors of bombs named *Little Boy* and *Fat Man*.

Coat of Arms

The two swordfish in the market are gawked at by all
    who pass. Parents coax wide-eyed children up to ogle.
One grinning family has a photograph taken alongside.
    Picture these noble knights of the sea being caught,
their bodies, great muscles, writhing on the deck.
    The fish could be the heraldic sword-crossed emblem
of a family coat of arms, but their great lances
    are hacked off. All they could emblazon now
is the family *Homo sapiens.*

CLARA KRITIKOS

Accusation

You accuse me of standing on the soapbox of the daily news
     ranting against war gods, the gutting of Gaia, say I abuse
Mnemosyne's nine daughters, the fragile muses. I bear witness
     naturally to what is wrong, the distress
of everyday, mundane battles, whatever troubles us,
     be it Ares or the likes of Drudgerius, Domesticus, Mortus.

Ostraka

The eight winds blow,
an earthquake shakes Mount Olympus, cholera
ravages the states, drought everywhere, the mysterious
death of bees throughout the country,
the flowers and crops die, the hourly
slaughtering of innocents,
                        and all we do is debate
in the assembly, cast ostraka—shards of democracy—
regarding our ships, the color of their sails.

DANICHORUS

New Ostia

The red glow of the burning city towered into the sky.
The fetus of terror stirred in us. To witness people in flames
leap from high windows, call out. Too much.
The old world brought down around our heads.
The aftermath a seething bewilderment.
Tribunes fan the sparks of public anxiety
into panic, dispatch soldiers to ports, stations,
set up roadblocks, search for weapons. Rumors
of another attack. Opposition cowed by accusations
of being soft, unpatriotic. Special measures called for.
A supreme commander set up
to combat threats, terrorist legions.
How a timorous population can be molded.
Powers ceded to our Pompey Magnus
and his cronies, lining their already lined pockets.

The Bombshell

Helen: *I never went to Troy; that was a phantom.*

Euripides, *Helen*

Those within the inner circle knew the story. Even sane,
     family-man Odysseus toed the line after his ruse to dodge
the draft—casting salt for seed, feigning madness—was exposed.
     He shied from leading his men on another assault
to satisfy old brutal ways for the sake of a bombshell.
     Menelaus and the general assembly pumped up the demos,
the statesmen preying on their sense of impotence.
     Many declared the gods decreed this war to lighten
Gaia's burden, the weight of ever-increasing humans.
     A nation played its part—converting a lie into truth.
Blind shrewd Homer played his harp to that fabricated story.
     The phantom that launched a thousand missiles.

Fragment from the lost poem *Helen*

66

Another Empire

In notes to an old poem, the Seleucid Empire is mentioned.
      An empire that was hot on the tongues of its denizens.
Its fame spread thousands of leagues. Foreign dignitaries feared
      and bowed to it. All hailed Emperor Hegorgebus,
who, according to the notes, was thought of in later times
      —in the cold horology of the universe, which is quicker
than soon—as a short-sighted, perverse numbskull under
      the thumb of every consul, praetor, general, and goon
breaking coffers, squandering revenue on the military
      while folk starved, the infirm left without care.
Still the demos went on glorifying him, their imperial buffoon.

Odysseus

I tried to finagle my way out of another
    manufactured military campaign, but what could I do
when that wiseacre, Palamedes, cast my son
    in the path of my plough team? The tears of my boy,
on being manhandled, turned from fear
    to grief. I consoled Telemachus, said I'd not be gone long,
that he was boss now. What I missed most on the windy plains
    of Troy amid the debacle, the death of friends,
the infamous voyage back, was my laughing boy
    with the honey-brown eyes, the pillow fights, the games
of tag, football, letting him pip me in the hoop race.
    When I did arrive back to my son, the man,
it was right that I should approach him disguised as a beggar.

Fragment from the lost poem *Telemachus*

Being Human

To bystanders it seems I must decide between one
       man or another: Menelaus, companion
of a score of married years whose sound nature fortifies me,
       or the intimacy with the other in body. But the one
I'll choose will not be the one, for as soon as I pick one I miss
       the other. Both glasses half empty.

Fragment from the lost poem *Helen*

Father Abroad

I avoid places where children play:
    squares where families congregate; parks
with swings, slides, monkey bars, seesaws;
    the seaside where yesterday I turned my head away
seeing a father and mother with their kid, the dad
    running, pretending not to be fast enough to catch up
with his laughing child. My Telemachus, my son,
    you tag me everywhere I turn.

Fragment from the lost poem *Telemachus*

Life

When a god is against you it's bad enough,
but when you're far from home, alone,
what hope have you? I found him gasping in the surf.
I tended his wounds. I told my story, he his.
It's in the intimacy of our stories: the troubles
of childhood, family, daily battles that set off
the bonding neuropathways, the byssus
that unites lovers, as much as the solace of bodies
together. I, of course, wanted him to stay,
for us to tie the knot, love on his guilt-wracked face,
fretting about his wife, his household. We leaned
against the portal of hope. Still, when Hermes showed up,
ordered me to let him go, I obeyed for his sake.
I helped him build the raft. We wept.
He yearned most for what he couldn't have, daft
as any mortal. He had to go. Nothing else to know.

Fragment from the lost poem *Calypso*

71

Parents

What do any of us know about our parents,
      separate or together? My mother kept the house
in order, prepared food, wore the epinetron smooth
      rolling the threads, the skeins of daily love.
She wove our clothes, played knucklebones, snakes & ladders,
      lined up with other women at the well,
walked home balancing the vase on her head
      as she balanced our family, the oikos.
Like most parents she hid her care, the arguments
      with my father heading off on another odyssey.
Da played dead when I stabbed him, let me
      wear his helmet, turned into a tickle monster.
Ma scolded him for exciting me before bed.
      I suppose they were like most parents. What do I know?
I had no others. They were mysterious as the night sky, the god
      hidden within the dark of the forbidden inner temple.

Fragment from the lost poem *Telemachus*

FRANCES THE PRIESTESS

Go-Between

Forgive your fighting parents the post-argument silence game
assigning you go-between, their Hermes, till tension thawed:
"Tell your father dinner's ready," etc. Always the same.
Give thanks to them—eschew casting any blame—
for making you their ankle-winged, fleet-as-thought god.

PEITHO

The God of Married Sex

More than any other god this one plays second fiddle
      to the busy hubbub of modern life,
for all our preoccupation. Call him Himeros or Pothos.
      We hardly give him the time of day,
compared to Mammon, or the god of drudgery.
      We maybe squeeze in a quick prayer to him
before sleep at night, perform the rite. Go through the motions.
      We should pay him more respect, grant him more time.
If not, he'll set the Erinyes of discontent on us.

The Divorced Mother

Today you are Demeter, unable to eat, hair undone,
    holding a torch for your daughter. You go to the ends
of the earth for her, the earth itself in sympathy.
    You grieve not for half a year, but half a week
each week your child spends with Hades.
    And it isn't that your ex is that bad a guy,
it was just you found his company infernal
    in trivial ways, and not just when he forced his body
on you, revisiting that day you picked flowers in Enna.
    You harvest your free time; sometimes yearn so much
for your child, you long to be back in the place of asphodels,
    to dwell again in the security of family.

ANTONIUS THE ELDER

Humilities
for Anna

You know the story. Zeus and Hermes came down
     to earth. No one took them in except an old couple.
Philemon set the table while Baucis
     prepared the meal: smoked bacon, vegetables
from their garden, feta and radishes, a dessert
     of apples and walnuts. The married pair realized,
noticing the amphora mysteriously full after each pour,
     who was under their roof. What's unknown is
that they begged the gods not to send the deluge on
     their inhospitable neighbors. It was they who outshone
the miffed deities then. Ah, the wisdom of old age,
     the humility to not care about one's own humility,
to be beyond the scruples of gods and mortals.

Goddess of the Hearth

And what about Hestia? We know little of her story.
    Where's the record of Penelope
and Telemachus playing checkers before the fire?
    Or the version in which Odysseus escaped the draft,
never left for Troy, enjoyed the solace
    of arriving home after work, pouring a glass of wine,
romping with his boy, having given thanks to the goddess?
    Hestia, as unassuming as so many wives, husbands,
parents slaving at chores without a word
    of thanks, feeding the hearth, the embers rekindled.

Concealment

A man walked past. We practically
     brushed shoulders, the lane was so narrow.
I nodded, muttered a *Kalimera*, but
     he chose to look ahead, ignore me.
I've seen that look, that demeanor before,
     always in rural towns, villages:
Toome, Morrisville, Derrynane, Delphi.
     Not simply the buttoned-up look that is the result
of living in a small community,
     but the face that stubbornly shuts out the invasion
of sightseers, yuppie realtors, outsiders.
     It conceals the gold bar of butter,
rancid or no, left buried in the bog,
     safe from any museum,
the last salted treasure of the lost world.

GRADIUS

Back in the Old Country

We are armed with cameras, guide books, maps;
     ready to grasp the spirit of antiquity
that's like a slain emperor
     propped up on his saddle,
his horse whipped back into the battle's fray,
     convincing even his own side he's still alive.

The Green Line

Of all the roads, including the breathtaking cliff routes
    of Parnassus, the Healy Pass, or Coomakista,
the type we love most are those roadlings
    off the beaten track with grass breaking through
the tarred center, a green line: the one down to our house
    from the Pass of the Treasure, or the Serpentine Way,
where you might see a yellow bunting, kingfisher, or badger.
    The grass is a sign, a grassroots demonstration
led by Gaia, or Dana declaring "We shall overcome" or
    some such cliché. The daisies and dandelions shoot up
through asphalt, flowers stuck in the muzzles of guns.

Resort

The ocean wraps its surf scarf round the shoulder
of the shore. Everything's in touch with everything else:
    the sky with the sea, the wave susurrus
with the zephyr in the fuchsia and furze, the cock crowing
    again and again, dawning on us
every second is now. And then the daytrippers come,
    I among them, a scout,
already parked. The army of cars winding along the road
    glitters like the helmets of hoplites,
takes over for a while, the legions
    of an empire going the way of all empires.

At Home

We are weary of the bounty of beauty,
      the terraced steps of terracotta-roofed houses,
trendy shops, cute domed chapels, picturesque harbor
      with its island castle and old-fashioned schooner.
This town's still not overwhelmed by the tourist industry.
      On the verge maybe, but saved today
by a shabby tanker that could do with a fresh coat of paint.
      The merchant ship gives the place perspective,
rusty relief from the rustic past. The modern
      ugly we've become accustomed to, yearn for,
helps us feel at home in all this antique splendor.

Foreigner

Good to be a stranger in a city, swan about
    its streets, lanes, quays, establish headquarters
in a café or tavern, get to know the regulars
    but not long enough to see their other sides,
or be taken for granted. You, the fresh slate, the tabula rasa.
    Everyone seems so amiable. The character who wears
his cap at a rakish angle, the geezer with his young wife,
    the chatty woman dressed in clothes too young for her.
Observe them tenderly: tipsy Pan, aging Aphrodite
    in short skirt, Zeus in from the rain,
his umbrella blown inside out, cursing "Boreas, that ass,"
    Leda giving you the eye—look out, trouble there.
Nothing like hobnobbing with the local pantheon.

The Mechanic

In a one-donkey town, Pyrgos, we drive to a garage
      glimpsed at the last T-junction, deflated as our tire.
In the doorway the mustached mechanic
      sits on a crate, as though waiting for us.
I point to the flat, indicate we've no spare.
      He jacks the car up, unscrews the bolts,
extracts the wheel damaged on the rim, hammers it
      good as new, mends the puncture,
bolts the wheel back, all without a word
      between us and in less than five minutes.
Maybe this god of mechanics considers a puncture
      beneath his dignity. I'm inclined to think
he prefers that his oily hands do the talking.
      He wipes them with a rag, grunts, turns away.

Heat Wave in Sitia

We take a break from the African heat under palm trees
    with boles like giant pineapples that line the harbor.
The whitewashed houses scramble
    on each other's shoulders to catch sight
of the water, a ship on the horizon, bathers,
    fishing boats, the wavelets like fans
cooling the shore, the Attic woman in a black peasant shawl
    fanning her heat-wrinkled face. Her stoical gaze
says we've seen many days like this. We have survived.

Tiresias

In the hotel foyer I can't help but observe the receptionist
     isn't given a breather. People don't see that he's swamped
in paperwork. They are too absorbed in their hectic journeys.
     They bombard him with *Is it far*
to Parnassus? What's today's forecast?
     Where's the best bookstore? When's the next ferry?
He's as wise as he is kind. He answers each query,
     realizes it is better to yield to the barrage,
resigned to the Hades of tourism.

CHRISTOPHORUS SILENTIARIUS

The Third Voyage

for Bobysseus

Exhausted, we arrive in an out-of-the-way fishing town.
    The shabby hotel has the feel of a mariner's house.
Boats pass in the dark with their tilley lamps,
    and for a moment we think
that it is we who are on a moving boat
    as we watch the vessels motor out. In such a place
I fancy Odysseus planted his oar, tired of drifting.
    All he wanted was to be left alone, to settle
in such a foreign harbor, still
    have the illusion of being on water, of voyaging.
The best of both worlds, finding himself
    relieved from the demons of fame,
giving himself up to glorious anonymity.

Templenoe

The seine boats, colorful as jockeys, jockey each other
    at the starting line, with names like racehorses:
El Niño, *Rainbow Warrior*, *The Liberator*, *Challenge*,
    Golden Feather, *The Kingdom*. With a shot they're off.
The crowd lets out yelps, incitements subduing even
    raffle sellers, ice cream van jingles, trinket stalls.
The holy gods of Tackiness are beaten for now by local gods
    inciting crews to win: the stocky helmsman of Waterville,
the shrewd one of Valentia, the determined one of Derrynane.
    The silver trophy glitters on Templenoe Pier, winks
that the gods of antiquity are with us still. Make no mistake
    about it. On Iveragh. Which one will lift the cup today?

Trailer

Something about the quality of sea swaying in the bay at Hydra
    calls to mind the crowd in the Savoy Cinema long ago,
swaying in unison as everyone sang along with the organist,
    words rising line by line on the screen. We've forgotten
the name of the organ man, famous in our town
    at the earth's center. We've forgotten the lost world
of singalongs—singsongs we called them—gone the way
    of cold type, horse troughs, a particular texture of bread,
certain words. But right now everyone's swaying side
    to side, a great moving sea in an antique land.

KINCELLAS MAJOR

Weather Relief

After days of unusually fine weather, a cloud
     settles like a hood on the peninsula, shuts out
this renowned ragged coastline:
     mythical islands, beaches, windy roads, tropical flora.
We're relieved of the sense something in us can't
     match its unsettling splendor, that life
now is more clearly bearable,
     that we're more at home on this cloud-shrouded shore.

CONNECTINUS

Good Company

The water washes up around a rock like a wind-blown
        wedding veil, a child's hand in a passing car waves
to a waving whitethorn bush, the turquoise of shoreline sea
        and deeper teal far out are highlighted by the sun,
my smile reflects in your shades. Ah, nothing exists
        without another. It's good not to be alone, be alive even,
better anyway than yesterday, that grey mist
        like a drear god descended and made nothing
of everything. Nothing. But forget that now. Yesterday
        is defined only via today and today thankfully
via yesterday: everything made out of nothing rather
        than nothing made out of everything.

DAVIDUS MELBURNIUS

Vinegar

Oh, the gasping straw-colored landscape
     of southern Crete, the parched mountains
—with modest adobe, ruby-domed chapels
     like weather stations on the mountain crowns—
crawl down on their knees to the sea, begging for water,
     just a drop, a sip to quench their thirst.
The big drink sniggers and offers them salt
     as Jesus was offered vinegar
while the soldiers played dice beneath,
     not giving a damn one way or other about the god
above them as he beseeched His Father
     to forgive them, that they know not what they do.

The Apostle in Corinth

And so Paul proselytized in this place, the remains
      we stand upon below the limestone mountain,
Acrocorinth, with the hodgepodge fort
      harboring also the temple of Aphrodite,
the hotspot of call-girls who satisfied the local swells.
      From here, he established the condemnation of the body
long before Augustine, chastising those buckos
      for profligate ways. What's not recorded is that he envied
their dedication to the flesh, shunning the thought
      that this was simply healthy fun, afraid of his predilection.
He fled, not because he gave up on the Corinthians,
      but for fear he'd surrender to appalling desire.

Sermon

...we have a savior who has been tempted in every way, just as we are—yet is without sin.

Hebrews 4:15

These days the Savior could not come back
to live without sin among us, the matrix beneath the surface
of daily existence being sewn so intricately
by that crafty dark angel, tireless Complicity.
God's temples are heated by oil secured at the expense
of slaughter. The pillows He'd lie on are the down
of the bird that saved Noah. Even sackcloth
would likely have molecules of blood in its stitches.
He couldn't drop down, mosey
around town, take in His handiwork: trees rising up
from concrete, the hubbub of folk about their workaday,
a passing woman who reminds Him of Magdalene, the smell
of coffee. How He envies the creature
created in His own image. How He longs to become His image.
How He pines for this earth. How absurd
the old God feels now. Our Image. Pray for Him.

Visiting the Church of Saint John of the Apocalypse, Patmos

Almost lunchtime. We enter the shining womb of the Church
    with its solid gold candlesticks, tabernacle,
utensils, icons painted by anonymous priests
    portraying the End. All the caretaker cares about is
shepherding us out, tired of people, this holy show,
    this apocalypse, impatient for his dog, couch, siesta.

Sleep

We're hardly aware of Hypnos in all his guises.
        Consider the siesta, saving us from overbearing Helios,
mundane care, permitting us to catch up after a night
        nursing a sick child. And what about the catnap
on a train, or over a book in a library?
        We wake up, the battery recharged,
all set to burn midnight oil, dance, court, lift
        a glass with Dionysus. If we're sensible
we'll treat Hypnos properly, allow him his third of the day
        to treat our wounds, call in the Oneiroi,
the psychedelic boys, the dream-makers to guide us
        through the magic mirrors, the surreal film
beneath our fluttering eyes, watching over our repose,
        before we shake ourselves free, face another day.

PHIONA

Our Times

When exactly we felt it we can't say, a tiredness beyond
    any we felt before, beyond age, beyond acedia,
beyond work, beyond burning the candle, beyond megrim
    and malinger. Our blood is mercury. We are heavy
as the cadaver of ourselves, lugging our own dead weight,
    a condensed black star, a tar-star
traveling night years, dropping uranium-dense tiredness,
    tiredness made night, exhausted night, weary night.

To Night

The god of day, Diurnus, is more than usually relieved to see
     the god of night descend. He says,
"I couldn't wait for you, old Nocturnus.
     I'm weary of bipeds, such a shady bunch,
always pulling the blinds. I'll take to my bed, sick of making up
     tomorrow's to-do list, fixing the alarm clock,
insisting there's hope, that tomorrow is
     another day. I'll take another nitroglycerin tablet
to ease chest pain. Perhaps the hour has come for me
     to give in, to hand myself over to you, say Good Night."

EAMONNUS

Dawn

Waking, the sky clear, a few gray wisps
    of cloud in the firmament,
the only hint that the avuncular god of night
    was here, puffing away
on his clay pipe, all reverie I imagine,
    feet up, comfy, at ease
at last, watching over us, not wanting to wake us,
    his poor clay charges, too early, slipping off
on soft-falling moccasins of light.

Birth Notice

This morning, mindlessly doing a marriage chore,
    making our bed, the smudge of your blood
on the white linen sheet wasn't the folklore
    of the seal of freshly opened womanhood,
but, rather, the branded red wax impression,
    sealing another month's quiet depression,
the privy stamp of childless parenthood.

ELIZÁVETH GRAMMATICA

Breakfast

Sip by sip Poseidon is away,
    the ebb tide emptying the bay,
leaving cappuccino suds along the strand
    sprinkled with cinnamon of sand.

On the Make

Sunday morning, the train emerges not just from the tunnel
    of Penn Station, across from the Catacombs,
the Palisades, the shining lordly Hudson, but from the hell
    of another excursion to hustle for my poems.
Enough. Head north to my hermitage.
    Know again the rapture of the pen across the page.

Lulu's Family Diner

I'm lucky enough to get a window seat
      overlooking the mountains, north of Adamsville Plain.
The landscape is a platinum blonde, dyed by fall.
      Lulu hums a Country song, serves me home fries
the shade of the countryside, tells me to make myself at home.
      Lulu is the beautiful muse of what they call homely.
I think I have a crush on her. She returns, asks
      if I want a refill. I tell her the home fries were the best
ever. This makes Lulu, lonely Lulu, lovely Lulu, happy.
      Not many can say they made a muse feel good.
Not many can say a muse called them "Honey."

To a Poet Friend

The door of our home is always open.
    Everyone knows the key is under the rock.
We never ask for thanks, being glad
    friends are there, finding a refuge.
Rancor rose in one seeing the house above the ocean,
    the islands named after gods, the lush wood,
garden, my happy wife and child stacking turf
    like gold bars against the side wall,
the cherry floors, wainscoting, books, some with my name
    on the cover: my life thus far that my writer friend
leafed through, faulting me for all I'd done,
    or rather for all he hadn't, failure
by comparison. I said nothing. I wanted to tell him
    I feel I've achieved little also, but
to say this would have irked him all the more.
    He left to be among those who've given up.
He's gone to join the failure club.

The Small Picture

to Heanius and Christophorus Silentiarius

The priest rambles on about how we're each a particle of sand,
    —such a tiresome analogy—that we each imagine
a grain in the light between thumb and index finger
    not unlike the way I hold my pen now.
I almost spoke up, said he's making too much of us,
    that this grain of sand is more like our star, our sun.
Consider then a speck too small for the eye to see, our earth.
    Then imagine ourselves in the big picture. Yes,
I know the story, but today your few words of praise
    —what does it matter what you praised?—
made me forget my smallness. Puffed me up.
    Comedic as it sounds. Who knows,
it may be true. Who knows, we all may be worthwhile. Imagine.

Dropping Names

To go unnoticed is good, though mostly we forget
        and silently crave attention, fame,
to be seen, adored even, above all others—unseemly.
        Listen to rain's patter on your hut
away from everyone. If you have any need to drop a name
        then hobnob with the likes of demigod Solitude
or the irenic deity of the rain, an unseen local god
        whose name's long forgotten, or is unknown.

DAVIDOS BARBAROS

Arion's Retribution

On the voyage home the other sailors coveted his poetry prize. As they were about to kill him, his song drew dolphins to the ship that bore him to safety in Taenarum.

His best days were there on Taenarum, startled
 to be still alive, finding his bearings,
kneeling in the morning grass embrocated with dew,
 wondering at the lambent eyes
of creatures at night, the nervy rustle of animals
 in the woods, the lizards lolling
under the sun, the general pellucid light
 sparkling on the quartz rock, Apollo's encomium.
He knew then the contiguity of all his eyes fell on
 during his exile, when folk took him
for dead. This was his halcyon time, turning misfortune
 into felicity, such a critical survival skill.
         But it was not
until recuperated, in need of company
 and retuning to Corinth, that he realized this boon.
Arriving in the capital, not without regret
 and reservation, he told his story to the court.
Though in this variant—for this has happened before
 and to other Arions—he bade Periander to stay his hand
when the ship of laureled fellow sailors
 strutted into town thinking they were home
and dry. He said, "Perianth, do not condemn them to Hades,
 rather allow me to stand before them on the proscenium
and lavish gratitude with my song hoard, for it was only

by virtue of their foul play that I was blessed with this word-booty on the bounteous isle of Taenarum."

To Those in the Shade

Let us speak of the partners, wives, husbands
    and children of the limelit ones.
Penelope rather than Odysseus, the wives
    of the gallivanting apostles, their daughters and sons
left behind or dragged all over Galilee,
    the forgotten husband of Lesbia
to whom she dedicated poems long since lost.
    Or Arion's wife who cooked his meals,
washed his clothes, made sandwiches
    as he set off on another reading tour,
putting up with his tantrums, his bouts
    of writing under the spell of a new muse,
his petty jealousies in the literary arena,
    the poets jockeying to ride Pegasus into the ground.
Praise all those in the shade of the limelight.

These Days

It's another sign of the end—as much say
    as the return of the old empire run by an ignorant but
not quite dumb Demos, or the bought-off media chorus—
    that everyone poets-about, brandishing books,
sporting poet certificates on tenured walls, gathering in schools,
    filling the latest definitive anthologies
with each other, scratching one another's backs with awards.
    They are too afraid to laud another camp
or praise the odd loner who is not a part of any pack
    and who is as endangered as the tiger, seldom seen,
lumbering through the daily-diminishing forest.

PAVLOS KERRIUS

The Literary Party

I gave you the gift of a book
with a cover that you could judge
the inside by, a hand casting
a world conjured with ink magic.
You opened the present, said nothing,
hardly a thank you. I, who took
so much time, delight and trouble
to give you this. To add salt,
you lavished praise on other gifts,
some of them flashy tinsel.
I slipped off my paper crown,
stepped out into the dark, head down.

The Era of Busy

The drudgeries of another day ticked off the list,
      the palimpsest already filling with tomorrow's chores.
We barely keep our snorkel above the relentless waves
      of busy-ness in an era that, according to the soothsayers
of our childhood, we'd be awash with oceans of time,
      what with computers, mechanization.
But my first chance of a few free moments
      —allowing me a quick read of short poems, and
to jot this on the back of tomorrow's list—is waiting in a bar
      for a friend who thankfully is late. I call for a beer.
The muses, with little time to ambush me, must strike swiftly.
      They're the resistance, partisans from Helicon. The foam
of a few moments to myself overflows the frosted glass.

Master Tardy

Late again. Another train missed. The doors shut in your face.
　　　You leave everything to the last second, never one
to waste time waiting, you waste it even more consigned
　　　to the waiting room; vexation and frustration turn
to acedia. The Spirit of Punctuality is out to teach you a lesson.
　　　Even kings are sentenced to schedules, timetables.
You're under the thumb of tyrant Tardy. He'll be the death
　　　of you. All you'll be early for is your own funeral.

The Good Die Young

This cliché-maker winces at his remark
      having become a maxim. He complains that he blurted
this hogwash to parents whose daughter drowned herself,
      that his consolation sprang from being at a loss
for words of comfort. He thought better of all the souls
      who fumble through to middle age, worn down
by the path alternating mostly between rocky way
      and mulch; bonds and hopes that seemed infrangible
sagging like torn twigs, leaves at half mast, snapped stems;
      the branch-backlash of lover or friend forging ahead;
energy declining to velleity, exhaustion even in the vales
      of joy or the brief clearings of the day.
You, who have left the groves of youth,
      struggling through the gnarled wood of middle age,
the muddy-floored forest of the elder,
      laud yourselves now, the good who muddle on.

THOMAS THE GARDENER

Understory

Redwood sorrel adapts so well to light levels
    that its heart-shaped leaf
folds down and hides under direct sunshine,
    opens up in shade, diffused rays. We're not
unlike that plant, never getting far from earth,
    hardly able to take the fierce light of joy,
or bliss, nor the pitch night
    of despair or fear. We survive best
in the shadows, the understory of our days.

ANTONEL OF CARRUCIUS

To Another Daily God

Today I want to thank the daily god of unhappiness,
        petty worries, disgruntlements, sorrows great
and small, for having taken such good care of me,
        making himself at home in my days,
and for taking the odd break as now he slips away
        into the background, smiling kindly perhaps,
giving me over to his reclusive sibling, Peace,
        at a traffic light on Pearl and Union. The sun
softens the snow-bordered street, the ice-cased lake.
        We turn into our clearer selves like snow and rime
turn to water. I wave a driver ahead. He avidly
        waves thanks. I would like to wave
gratitude to the god of unhappiness.
        He could've finished me off often enough.
His present absence highlights my happytime.

In Praise of Failure

Make no mistake, it's good to get the thumbs down,
        spared the crowd singing your praises when their flattery,
their cheers take their cue from the reviewing heads of the day
        signaling their fancy. We've got this wrong. Thumbs down
directed the winner to stick his sword in the ground, to not
        take the loser's life. I was fortunate to see the royal thumb
point down, to slip away, wounded, spurned, but still alive,
        released from the arena, free of responsibility,
favored by the emperor of obscurity.

A SELECTION FROM THE
ATHENIAN WORKSHOP PAPYRUS

The following five poems are from an exercise set by Gregory the Elder in the Athenian Workshop after the participants' night at a local symposium.

DANDIUS

Aubade

I didn't resort to the hair of the god
    that bit me. Being by the sea I went for a dip.
Afterwards I never felt better,
    my hangover dispelled by the trident deity,
the cold brine shocking the system out of its doldrums,
    soothing it, lifting it like a wave,
sparkling in the sun. Poseidon is a swell.
    Now I'm myself again, it's time to celebrate,
to raise a cup to you, Dionysus. Cheers. Your health.

ANONYMOUS, PROBABLY THE
YOUNG RAKIUS

PASU

(Post-Alcoholic Sexual Urge)

This morning I woke at dawn—cock crow
    would be more correct, Chrysilla, after all
the vino yesterday. Wouldn't you know,
    you had no mind for a morning call,
my drinker's alarm clock, nudging you awake.
    And last night—my hot wife—
you were in the thrall of Himeros. But for Bacchus' sake,
    I had the wine-decline. Oh, drooping life.

COFFIUS

Cycles

Usually after periods of solitude, domesticity, work,
    I'm swept by the sense that something's missing,
another Antaeus touching down
    on the ground of the earthy, the flesh of mascara'd night,
the heavy breathing of seedy rooms and alleys,
    to be reminded that life is tastier
seasoned by the salt of anxiety, the pepper of guilt.

GRIGOROSKEPTIS

The Nine Fluffers

The muse lifts wilting songs. She's like a fluffer
     between takes in the shooting of a porn show,
keeping the studs alive, hard, erect, tumescent.
     Art is closer to sex than we think, like it or no.

COLMOS GAELICUS

The Artist's Disgrace

The player strums, tires of what he loves
     to do, plays from the graveyard of his self
for a few drachma. Local muses revive him.
     Let not the music of this place
suffer such disgrace, the bouzouki itself pregnant
     on its back, patiently waiting to give birth.

The Most Neglected God of All

Now let us praise the most neglected god of all,
        the god of the Hand Job, Hand Shandy, Master
Spank the Monkey, Madame Frig. The god
        that everyone: housewives, presidents,
gurus, Zen monks—so that's the One Hand Clap—rabbis, nuns
        have been possessed by, ever since it was handed down
to Pan who in turn handed it on to shepherds. The god Atum,
        whom the Egyptians say gave rise to us all.
Not The Big Bang then, but The Big Hand Job. The god
        pouts that we never pay him public due.
We're ashamed, embarrassed at having lit
        a furtive candle to him. Myriads down
through the ages have attended his daily secret service
        wherever the members of his church could find:
offices, buses, alleys, bathrooms, beaches, cars.
        There's hardly a spot on earth
people haven't laid their offering. What's the strangest place
        you've communed with this handy god? Even as we speak,
millions of hands are busy all over the world.
        You yourself may have been blessed by him today.
Have you given thanks? Enough of turning a blind eye,
        of being small, stunted. Come now.

The Ladykiller

Suddenly, catching myself in the mirror,
     —hard to figure what precipitated this shift,
appropriately in The Old Town Bar—the timeless self-image
     of a curly, handsome twenty-something-year-old
fell away before my eyes and I saw this unfamiliar
     gray-haired chap, hair receding above his temple.
Only this morning, the world at my feet, I was God's gift
     to women, a ladykiller. The Graiae, three crones
born white-haired, nudge each other on nearby stools.
     My new girlfriends flirt with me, only one tooth
between them in their snickering heads.

Prayer in Summer

Now I realize what's up on this sunny day: women
    with hardly a stitch on, all shapes and sizes,
almost all beautiful, or rather a turn-on, grace the streets
    and I'm without energy to maneuver the chat-up
at bus stop or shop line as I deftly managed, it seems now,
    in the testosterone days, finding myself sooner
rather than later lost in another's body. Now I wish
    the Hades of winter back, Persephone safely wrapped up,
the street in a heavy overcoat of prickly woolen snow.

Amen

The waitress leaned over the table
     next to us, in a low-cut blouse
and I was the boy at the first jingle
     of the consecration bell, my head
bowed prayerfully, beating my chest.
     As the raised God, made flesh,
was held on high for the second time
     I couldn't help
myself. I just had to look. Amen.

The Goat

When you reach to help the hurt creature,
 it usually reacts in fear
—what does it know of goodwill? Remember
 that day on Coomakista Pass
the goat that had trapped its head
 in a wire box fence. No matter
from what angle we patiently approached,
 it bucked,
the wire cutting into its neck all the more
 till finally we gave up. The memory
of that goat returns, I
 being in the grip of old ways,
old goat ways I never
 seem to slip free of, helpless
to untangle goathead, desperate
 to hold to that one security.
At least this he knows. At least this
 is certain.

Tug of War

Right now the old conventional tug of war goes on.
    The Pheromones versus the Choice team.
The thigh muscles bulge, faces strain puce.
    The sweaty heroic battle.
Exhausting. The best we can expect is
    the Choice side holds, and not allow
the other side—Boozing Bill, Delia Dope,
    Dusty Lust & Co—to drag them, the underdogs,
over the line till they lie beaten, grimacing in the dirt,
    the Pheromones doing a lap of honor, brandishing
the cup, cheering, gloating through every cell of the body.

Addict

I'm like those dolphins
       I read about, confined in isolated cells
             of a pool with sliding doors.
A zoologist manipulated their encounters,
       observed their sexual behavior.
The one released dolphin
       refusing to take to the sea,
             head-butting the pool's gate to get back in.

Beach Wish

A blind couple, hand in hand, tap their way along the boardwalk.
    Hardbodies laid out on the golden altar
of the body-beautiful check each other out.
    Look at that shining Adonis, this bikini'd Helen.
It isn't good to test the gods, be granted what is wished for,
    but now I envy this couple, their unseeing sight.
Neither one is a looker. What does that matter? They see better
    in their way, free of the look in vogue, that tan body,
those muscular thighs, that hourglass figure
    telling the time, the despot of fashion focusing the eye.

Benefits of Age

A young woman strolls out of the below-zero
    weather, breasts nippling her T-shirt. You let her go.
A benefit of sagging age. You relax into
    the day, enjoy being alone, the hush of vestal white snow
outside the glass doors, the hustle
    into the manufactured warmth of the mall,
this Western bazaar with its Christmas carols, holiday bustle.
    Good to be in control, not at pheromones' beck and call.

ANONYMOUS

Escaping the Party

Our eyes meet and hold. The alcohol is a potion,
        freeing inhibitions, forgetting we're married
but not to each other. We escape to an out-of-the-way bar.
        Kissing, our tongues flicker
in and out of one another, flames of votive candles
        at a side-altar, praying for a miracle,
released from concern, responsibility.
        The wax of intermingling candles
weeps below the beatific, sorrowful face,
        the merciful patron saint of adulterers.

Buoyancy

In Mesopotamia couples suspected of adultery
      were tied together and thrown in the river.
If they floated they were innocent, set free.
      If they sank: guilty.
You worry about what folks think. But every culture
      has laws of buoyancy.
Don't worry. I'm a good swimmer,
      in my element in water.
Be still, relax your body
      bound to mine. We won't go under.

Another Version

Hephaestus tried to ravish Athena, but she fled and his seed spilled on the Acropolis.

This afternoon you were Athena on the balcony
    in a short black dress, commando style.
Your open tanned thighs revealing the only shrine
    I kneel to lately. But today my adoration, my come-on,
was repelled. You weren't in the mood.
    I was the deformed god making my advances.
But this time you showed a modicum of sympathy, Athena,
    letting down your shoulder strap, raising your dress a tad.
A flashing goddess. I, Hephaestus, spurted on
    the ground below the Parthenon, a relieved voyeur.

Return

Unable to stop ourselves, we parked off the road in Arcadia,
      clambered down into the copse. Everyone is overcome
by the gods from time to time, possessed by them, like it or no.
      Then I was Pan, goatee and all. You were Syrinx,
but this time you didn't make a bolt for it,
      didn't turn yourself into a reed.
We made out in that bug-infested sacred grove,
      assisted by last night's Viagra.
We managed to ignore the pestering insects,
      the traffic flashing by on the road to Sparta.

"Try Again, Dolt"

We spiced up the lust of our living dust
     watching ourselves in the mirror's blue movie,
pistoning in and out... Forgive us, Eros, our failure,
     who simply want sullied words to praise you,
releasing us from the quotidian: our workaday,
     the prolonged winter, the snow
falling outside as though you yourself tore up
     this page and cast it into the air,
saying, "Try again, dolt, to praise the act,
     the glory of the friction of the bodies sparking off
each other like chips of flint, blazing up
     in the winter wilderness, in the ancient way."

Safety

The rapture on her face
    had the look of the prophesying Pythia,
narcotic fumes rising from the chasm below,
    inducing trance. When a god enters a body
the mortal is annulled, put out of misery.
    What a compliment Aphrodite paid me,
to feel safe in my company, to come down to earth.
    We were too frenzied to undress.
Besides, even a goddess is more inviting
    when a little is left to the eyes of the imagination,
her flexed calf muscles highlighted by blood-red stilettos.

Headway

In the early days nothing would stop us
    from fanning the brush of our lust into flame.
But as always with development we have grown less
    spontaneous. You say men are turned on the same
as gas flame, women like the slow starter of an electric ring.
    Let us make flint of our bodies once more, light
with that primitive spark. Not all progress is advance.

Mercy

The attractants raced like a riotous mob, usurping self-rule,
    the congress of flesh through partly open clothes.
We were beyond caring if the waitress noticed
    two flushed people entering the restroom.
Afterwards the Erotes relinquish control,
    take a breather as we order coffee and you bury
your head back in your book and I in mine,
    as if nothing happened, and twenty years pass
and I mutter something about how awful
    to be at the mercy of the flesh, that frenzied groping.
Oh, my long-legged goddess of the loo.

Purgatory

I want you to tell me everything will be hunky-dory,
    perfect, not unlike the way I wanted the priests' stories
of Heaven to be true. Hell and Purgatory
    are more believable. There are no guarantees.
To ask for Heaven is to make a hell of Purgatory.

Payment

Great, the time-out of love-making, no
        doubt about that. I was lucky
to have experienced the body of Aphrodite
        —wearing merely a silky thong—for a night
or three. But there's payment for such good fortune.
        Sadness, Loneliness, Longing are like vultures
hovering over the god, Ecstasy, waiting to descend
        and pick the bones of Eros
even at the very first, tender, shut-eyed kiss.

GREGOR

Avaunt

for Elina Makropulos

And since we have separated for better
    and for worse, I'm in withdrawal
from love's heroin shot, tended by the downer gods
    congratulating each other, having plucked
our lovebug wings. They are like kids who rip the wings
    off butterflies, gleefully watch them flop inside a jam jar.
I'll not go on, not give that bunch the satisfaction
    of garlanding our misfortune as they bid the muse
of tragedy herself, Melpomene, to my side. Enough, avaunt.
    I feel just fine, sweet, cool, Prince Cheerful himself.

LANIUS

The Regimen

All day I followed the regimen, routine
to keep me buoyant, took my morning pills:
    vitamins, anti-depressants, no caffeine,
      read poems—spirit sustenance—sent emails.
I got out of the house, reckoned Apollo
      highlighting the snow would lift the down
         I'd been attempting to ignore. No go.
I joshed with Hermes, the postman, played the clown,
      humor being the refuge of a desperate man.
Struggled on, forced myself to exercise, a swim
      to induce a rush of natural morphine,
        the cells' opium, the endorphins to kick in,
           raise my spirits. Useless. Nothing more to do
           except face up, succumb to missing you.

Vow

At times I imagine you don't give a damn
      for me, that you're seeing a bronze Adonis.
You give in after drinks, let him
      have his way. You even enjoy it. There is
no doubt you think I (yours untruly) daily screw
      every woman from here to Timbuktu.
There's no one but you. Hand on cock, I swear this to be true.

The Rat

Bad enough to miss you, but to think of you
     with another. It's as though a rat
senses he's about to gnaw his way out of my chest,
     instinctively intensifies his efforts behind
my ribcage, tissue, muscle. Any minute now
     his whiskered chin will rip through my skin,
appear with my pulsating heart in his dripping fangs.

It's an Ill Wind that Blows No Good

But the reverse is true too.
     A good wind often blows some ill.
You were the good wind that blew
     the daily missing you. The wind blows still.

The Breakup Contract

Who'd have thought we'd come to this a year ago?
    I sang happy birthday, a mite tipsy, over the phone.
I gave you gypsy earrings, chiffon scarves, a ring. We were so
    sure of our future together. Now you're on your own.
Now I'm on my own. My present to you on this day
    is not to make contact with you in any way.

Meeting Again

A wound itches as it heals.
    Scratching will reopen the cut.
We met once more. Of course
    the wound bled.
Festered afterwards. But what
    a relief to let ourselves go, to tear
and tear at that love scab.

Later

I sit in the same square, in the same overpriced café,
    watch the same frantic stream
of people pass by, the same comic pigeons
    reminding me of the way everyone speed-walks
in silent movies. I browse my book, come across
    a poem with that familiar quote of Heraclitus,
that nobody steps in the same stream twice.
    You were here only a week ago.

KATERINA PHILIA

A Quiet Glory

to Antonel of Carrucius and Davus the Consul

You must hold on after all these years
        of natter about sport, pulchritude, family, work,
the state of the world. The repetition of wilting stories.
        When all else fails—Eros, family, work—
it has been faithful, supportive on bad days
        like the trellis set in the earth so that hardy climbers,
glories, can wind their way up. Without friendship,
        maybe the greatest of all glories, you'll not fully bloom.

Worth Remembering

The only army of the ruined Acropolis of Sparta now
      is the army of ants filing back and forth over the stoa,
the soldiers' mess hall, the sanctuary of Artemis Orthia
      where whipping contests to toughen boys were held.
Time isn't that bad after all. Sure, all good things
      end, but all dreadful things come to an end also.

GALIA OF ITHAKI

The Caryatids in the Acropolis

So when the ruling, puffed-up males
    boast this is Democracy's birthplace,
let them consider us, the silent stone females,
    faces erased, holding up the roof-beams of our race.

ADRIENNE

A Reading

The elder poet leaned on her walking cane,
        conjured sentences from ink with matriarchal authority.
Mnemosyne herself, issuing the truth, unearthing the memory
        of the injustice perpetrated by one group on another,
the wrong that could be defined by a single chromosome.
        You know the uninkable one I mean, too big for words.
The fingers of her hands that might be a woman's
        or a man's played unconsciously up and down the staff
as if playing the lute of poetry, dispelling difference
        even as she spoke of disparity. She was a conduit
of beauty and truth
                        until something broke, shifted, a change
        of attitude, the message overpowering the source.
It's hard to put a finger on, but suddenly the lute
        turned back to a stick, Mnemosyne turned into a man.
No one said a word. In this way the music
        her hand artfully mimed was diminished.

EVANTHOULA

The New Athena

If the gods are simply players within mortals
     then it's time to lay down my plumed helmet, spear,
the aegis of my goat-skinned shield with gorgon's head.
     I pit difference between peoples: the Egyptians, Turks,
Trojans, the States, igniting their battle cry,
     the gore glory of war. Now I must allow my wise side
to emerge from within you, to break the cycle. I'll have a word
     in the ear of Ares, my blood-thirsty brother.
Even he's weary. I must now solely be the deity
     within you who seeks an answer in conflict
without bloodshed, guardian of the small few who command
     with their stentorian voice "No more."

Fragment from the lost poem *Athena*

DAVUS THE CONSUL

Laughter

On Center Street, Skala, fuming with traffic,
    tired-faced mothers wheel prams, processions
of schoolchildren wave flags,
    commemorating another military victory
—Ares smiling smugly on his infants.
    Three old women chat outside
the laundromat. I haven't a clue about what
    they say, but it's mirthful. The woman
without spectacles breaks
    into laughter, bends over in stitches
with a heartiness I haven't heard for ages
    at whatever the others say.
They've taken everything from life, wear black
    for all the reasons women wear black.
They've outshone even their own god,
    the orthodox God that never laughed.
May the memory of these women, the three graces,
    be with me now and in the hours of our blackness.

Disarming

A middle-aged woman—plain you might say—strolls by
     our house. I was out of sorts, not long up,
but her serene smile, without saying a word,
     remarks: "Take in the sun on the lake,
the honeysuckle's pink fingers bursting into yellow flames,
     the traffic on North Avenue for once gone so quiet
you can hear the whirr of the hummingbird's wings
     reversing in midair." On another morning such serenity
would have vexed me, but there is something so natural
     about her demeanor. She doesn't notice me.
Disarmed, I let what bothers me go
     and think since there's no corresponding god
—the pantheon being all piss and vinegar—
     we must create a new order and call her
Tranquilia, Calmes, or promote Halcyon and tell Aphrodite,
     Ares, Artemis, even Zeus, to move over in
the pecking order, set her smack in the middle, the woman
     who breezes by our house this divine morning.

GALI METAPHRASTRIA

Patient

The snow has melted clean off the mountain.
    It's winter still. Yet another indication that Gaia
is in trouble, that things aren't sound.
    The rocky mountaintop shines
like the bald head of a woman after chemo
    who wills herself out of her hospital bed
to take in the trees, the squirrels, the commotion
    in the town, sip beer in a dive, smiles
to the child staring at her shining head, wishing
    it didn't take all this dying to love life.

Speaking Plainly

So few care in comparison to the many
      that it might as well be no one.
The sun glaring through the Cyclops' eye
      of the atmosphere wipes out frogs,
whips up hurricanes, melts behemoth bergs.
      Forget that spin of how even one person
or creature can alter the world,
      that a butterfly flapping its wings
or a leaping toad can set off a wonder-chain.
      For myriads now, too late.

Fathoming

Our child, our sprat, gazes across the sea, unable to fathom
    the teeming life beneath: cod, eel, shark, porpoise,
the clownish cuckoo wrasse that I never imagined
    could exist till hauling lobster off Scariff Island.
This iridescent body, no more than five inches long,
    dazzled in the wire pot.
Our tiller man dryly remarked "Ah, that's
    just a wee cuckoo wrasse. Worthless."
I knew I could never catch the rainbow wonder
    writhing there on the oily deck, a creature instantly
losing neon hues in this fishy upper world, dying under
    our scaled eyes. Ah, forgive us, wee cuckoo wrasse.

Well You Know This Fish

False cleaner fish mimic harmless cleaner wrasse:
    larger fish stop by for a routine wash;
a seeming symbiotic lick; the false fish
    tears into shocked flesh. Such brass.

The New Pastoralists

Good it is to get off the beaten track, to chance upon
     this untrodden realm: the mall of trees, fluttering pennants
of leaves and butterflies, wild flowers, the creek. Arcadia.
     The dragonflies are stretch limos chauffeuring spirits
of the natural world through the portals of our senses.
     The muse of the pastoral steps down the waterfalls
in a dashing white gown. She requests the makers
     to burst forth into idylls lauding her once more, especially
now that we mortally hurt her. The trees and water applaud.

MULDUNUS THE MAGISTER GRAMMATICORUM

The Word

Over Ithaca deep into the lush, hushed green
　　undulating forest toward Syracuse the sky blushed
with damask dusk—it takes more nimble
　　　fingertip word freshness on the lute of renewal
to transmute the mere gist of such a firmament.
　　　And I recalled a word
serendipity brought as I searched for another
　　in the lexicon thick as a Bible.
A word I'd never laid eyes on or heard before, mysterious,
　　plain beautiful to me in its inkself.
How can we see without a new word, a new god?

PANOS KINNELLUS

The Other

Time to raise a paean to the olive-green slugs:
mauve maggots, slime-emerald algae, dandruff-creamy worms,
who make nothing of the corpse. The diverse bugs
we turn our heads away from, the loathsome swarms,
the steaming dung dolloped on the soil that springs roses,
potatoes, tomatoes, the food on our tables. Doff our hats
to all the matter and mites we look down our snotty noses
upon. Admit that we are blind, stupid, bats
—praise the bats too—that we are the great ungrateful.
Give thanks, erect monuments to them, the other beautiful.

The Winner

The bluebottle reigns supreme now
      over the kingdom of carcass—
it doesn't matter to the fly if it's cow,
      rat, swan, salmon, human, or ass.
The bluebottle is a glimmering gem
      not on Death's, but on Life's diadem.

RICARDUS LAMBUS

Old Timers

One old fat geezer stretches his stone-studded, dewlapped neck
    towards the skyline on the Miami River's opposite bank:
the Jade Building, the Ambassadors, the Four Seasons,
    the Bank of America. The iguanas have come to Florida
to retire also. They have seen so many creatures, epochs come
    and go. These little dinosaurs take in rays
like the movie idols in the five-star hotel
    less than a hundred yards away. The stars baste slowly,
tanning around the pool, favored by the god of fame,
    the human need to create gods, brings gods down
to earth. The iguanas smirk from ear to ear.

Life

The taste of drink: the subtle tang of white wine,
    the bitter slug of stout, the burning nip of brandy,
the sour cut of beer, swigged, quaffed and sipped: life
    distilled or fermented, hitting the spot
with a taste of more, leaving an aftertaste,
    a lingering sense of the perfect.

BERNARDIUS SCHOLASTICUS

Another Time

A man plays a squeeze box in a pub that's one of the old types,
    lyceum of another time.
He braille-buttons the melodeon, squeezes life back
    into a worn tune. People jaw away around the bar,
pay no heed to this avatar, the air necromanced into music.
    Not even the player knows how good he is.
The tragedy now is not so much that nobody notices
    a god, but that even the gods don't know they are gods.

Wonder of Wonders

A girl cries. Her father beats her, convinces her she's dumb.
     She'll land back in that cave of herself again and
again for the rest of her life. Many are like mythical characters
     blindly returning to tackle whatever invisible monsters
brought them down long ago. Maybe the wonder
     of wonders of being alive—greater even than the lake
like a glittering shield, the leaves turning tangerine,
     bronze, ruby and so infinitely on—is, as yet,
we have not completely undone our world.
     And should we each manage to wrestle
our own particular Trauma to the ground and tame him,
     there is Thanatos—his natural father—waiting
at the end of it all, the Bigwig behind all the trouble.
     Time to give ourselves a pat on the back,
thumbs up, for not yet having blown ourselves sky high.

Time Travel

The subway train emerging out of the tunnel
    underneath the Acropolis zooms through the agora
right by the Stoa of Attalos, the temple of Ares,
    the Panathenaic Way, Zeus' joint, the Nymphaion,
the ground Plato walked, where Socrates was imprisoned,
    where Aristophanes pulled the leg
of Demosthenes, Euripides plotted his soap operas. Look here,
    the train emerges out of the underworld of the future.

The Traveler's Grace

Nothing like landing in a foreign city
    early morning. Preferably in weekday hubbub.
Everyone going about their business, lost in themselves,
    not a thought of how strange, foreign, alien their lives are.
How abnormal to think it normal to find ourselves
    on a spinning ball reeling around a star
at thousands of miles per hour from who knows where
    to who knows where. How outlandish.
I'm one of the sacred dead,
    released from the underworld
of the mundane, the banal. Behold the normal.